Contents

PEDAGOGICAL PRACTICES TO OPTIMISE YOUR TEACHING

DR DHEERAJ MEHROTRA

PREFACE

Pedagogical Practices to Optimise Your Teaching *is an idea and a conception to make learning a priority for schools globally. Effective pedagogical methods have a solid scientific background, are easily understood by those who implement them in the classroom, and are direct solutions to the stated learning requirements of the students.*

The book ideally defines an idea to explore learning as a priority within classrooms.

Best & Cheers

www.authordheerajmehrotra.com

I
Pedagogical Practices

Pedagogical Practice #1

Make some adjustments to the instructional jargon you use:
Imagine things in a new way. Lessons on the alphabet like "A for Apple," "B for Boy," and "C for Cat" are no longer popular with today's kids. They want the letter A for Android, the letter B for Blackberry, and the letter C for Cloud!

Pedagogical Practice #2

When writing on the blackboard, you should use different coloured chalk. Additionally, investigate the possibilities of practising with whiteboards and other coloured markers.

Pedagogical Practice #3

Dress professionally and always use a QUALITY PEN; never use an average pen as a cosmetic effect by hanging it from your neck.

Pedagogical Practice #4

Believe in gaining knowledge rather than imparting it!

Pedagogical Practice #5

Remember that above all else, you are a TEACHER, not a mathematics or physics teacher or any other subject!
And never lose your enthusiasm.

Pedagogical Practice #6

The youngsters should be allowed to work in partnerships, which are groups consisting of two people.
Let the two of them conclude each response on their own. The addition of partners brings us to eleven!
For every work item, homework assignment, and even question posed by the Instructor!

Pedagogical Practice #7

To spice up your classroom, try making some ANCHOR charts.

Pedagogical Practice #8

When you are in the classroom, you must always use an educational tool.

Pedagogical Practice #9

Explain the Pedagogical Practice that you are going to be using as content using the most current example possible.

Pedagogical Practice #10

Deliver pride in anything you deliver.

Pedagogical Practice #11

Get CONFIDENCE in yourself before you do anything else—and keep doing it!

Pedagogical Practice #12

In both teaching and lecturing settings, demonstrate enthusiasm and a wow factor.

Pedagogical Practice #13

Praise your CHILDREN in front of other people, but if you ever need to correct them, do it behind closed doors.

Pedagogical Practice #14

The knowledge should be delivered using examples, references, and live coverage of the facts.

Pedagogical Practice #15

Always make it a point to provide your children with at least ONE EDUCATIONAL LINK each and every day.

Pedagogical Practice #16

Tell a tale or provide information that will make people want to read your site.

Pedagogical Practice #17

Maintain a question on your "bucket list" that you want to ask your students at all times.

Pedagogical Practice #18

Greeting one another good morning with a touch of personalization, such as "Hi Ashish, how are you doing today?"
Using someone's first name is an effective way to create rapport.

Pedagogical Practice #19

Have a conversation with your pupils about what goes on in the classroom. Give kids the opportunity to take ownership and responsibility for their own academic achievement.

Pedagogical Practice #20

Always have faith in the innovations being implemented in the classroom. Make learning a pleasure for the children by using TOOLS that are interesting to them and that are used often.

Pedagogical Practice #21

Establish a list of guidelines for proper conduct in the classroom.
Allow each of the kids to proceed in the same manner.

Pedagogical Practice #22

Avoid behaving in a manner that is disrespectful. Give each youngster in the class your undivided attention and a patient ear.

Pedagogical Practice #23

To succeed in education, a classroom has to function like a party. If you treat your kids with kindness, respect, and curiosity, you will find that they will do anything for you.

Pedagogical Practice #24

Imagine Giving Your Classroom a New Look! The days are long gone when we used to think in terms of rows and columns. Let there be a face-to-face, circular discussion.

Seating is arranged in a half circle, and there are no backbenchers at all!

Pedagogical Practice #25

Make an emotional appeal to the children instead of trying to reason with them. Engage on a deeper level with them emotionally. Instil in them a resilient emotional state.

Pedagogical Practice #26

Develop your level of interaction and

participation with the kids in the class. Ensure that every youngster is familiar with you and has at least one response prepared.

At the very least once every week with your questions!

Pedagogical Practice #27

Apply the strategy of BRAINSTORMING to your situation.

To investigate whether or whether the approach of group learning results in improved learning.

Pedagogical Practice #28

RAPPORT and other NLP techniques should be used inside educational settings.

Anchoring, Building, Mirroring, and Matching are all part of the Visualization process.

Pedagogical Practice #29

Use MIND MAPS

to instruct and to go over the previously completed task.

Pedagogical Practice #30

Communicate with the kids, encourage them to write, and help them narrow their topic using a PROMPT!

Pedagogical Practice #31

It is essential to teach self-awareness in relation to knowledge. Establish a Routine for the Classroom and Stick to It.

Pedagogical Practice #32

Develop a Culture of Explanation rather than one based on Obtaining the Correct Response

Pedagogical Practice #33

Employ Methods of Questioning That Force All Students To Think And Respond

Pedagogical Practice #34

Create a "Wow!" moment for your students in the instructional setting.

educating in a way that will capture the attention of the audience. Deliver PRIDE & DELIGHT!

Pedagogical Practice #35

Target children that engage in disruptive behavior using individualized strategies. Recognize and honor the attention and interests of each individual youngster.

Pedagogical Practice #36

Don't educate hard; instead, teach smart.
Train Your Students to Be Street Smart!

Teach children in a method that is more to their liking, not yours!

Pedagogical Practice #37

Keep abreast of the changing times by acquiring new information, not only in your own field but in other areas as well.

Keep in mind that you are a TEACHER first and foremost, not just an instructor of English, mathematics, physics, or Hindi.

Pedagogical Practice #38

To be successful as a TEACHER, you need to have a global life plan!
IMPROVE

Check the lesson you just gave and see how it compares to what you've been doing since then.

Pedagogical Practice #39

Successful educators need to have a plan that can be summed up in one word:
VISION

To Bring JOY AND SATISFACTION TO THEIR STUDENTS!

Pedagogical Practice #40

Make an effort to summarize the 3Ks'.
KODO, KAGNE, and KAIZEN are the three pillars of the Japanese philosophy of continually thinking, doing, and developing.

Pedagogical Practice #41

Establish your presence in the cloud, and check to see that your Google numbers are up to date so that you may continually wow your audience. Maintain an active presence on social and professional networking platforms.

Pedagogical Practice #42

Utilizing the power that technology provides, you should propel your classrooms into the next higher orbit. Create online blogs in which students may remark on the learning result and *feedback from the previous day!*

Pedagogical Practice #43

Start out your session on an exciting and upbeat note by continually inspiring the students and arousing their interest. This will set the tone for the rest of the course.

Pedagogical Practice #44

Communicate the purpose of the lesson to the youngsters. Also make an effort to have a solid understanding of what the pupils already know. They should be honored for their brains and praised for the information they possess.

Pedagogical Practice #45

Before beginning instruction, there should always be some kind of warm-up exercise. This might include going about the classroom, such as asking every child in the class to go and shake hands with the child sitting next to them.

Add two rolls to your order, either way you choose!

Pedagogical Practice #46

Discuss the topic while using e-learning to investigate or give a film on MOTIVATION or AWARENESS. Then have a discussion about it in the classroom.

Pedagogical Practice #47

Applaud even the smallest steps toward overall development in the class.
Hey there, I couldn't be more thrilled to be in this classroom right now. Every single one of my pupils is one of a kind and exceptional.

I want each and every one of you to get a perfect score in this class!

Pedagogical Practice #48

Put your ego aside.
Be prepared to speak in a manner that is understandable by pupils.

Pedagogical Practice #49

Show some friendliness and courtesy.
Maintain a kind demeanor, and make an effort to get to know each individual pupil in your class.
VIP!

Pedagogical Practice #50

Close the digital skills gap by soliciting feedback from students and encouraging them to teach one another on how to make effective use of technology.

If you need any help with ICT or IT Skills, don't be embarrassed to ask the students for their input.

Pedagogical Practice #51

Take advantage of our presence on CLOUD through.

*The specialized websites Scribd.com, Webs.com, Instagram Podcast, and more like them
In addition to your presence on Facebook, you should also be active on Blogit, Linkedin, and Twitter.*

Pedagogical Practice #52

*Give some thought to your health.
Keep yourself hydrated and don't miss any meals since your*

It's possible that teaching will require you to stand for too long.

Pedagogical Practice #53

Always have a positive attitude whether attending arrangement lessons or substitute classes, and see the experience as an opportunity.

to get knowledge from your pupils and use that knowledge into your usual routine by using it as icebreakers.

Pedagogical Practice #54

It would be helpful to try to create high expectations for all of the pupils. They declare, "All of my

kids deserve 100% in my subject".

Pedagogical Practice #55

Make sure you are well-prepared and organized with the material, especially the chapter.

as well as the general progression of the discussions in each and every class. Never let yourself be unprepared.

Pedagogical Practice #56

Build a STRONG connection with the students: this should take precedence over things like taking attendance and scheduling time for conversations.

Pedagogical Practice #57

Bring your own water bottle, reference book, and markers with you to class if you want to fully experience the greatest moments in teaching without interruptions from other students or teachers.

Pedagogical Practice #58

Carry some candies with you in case there is a praiseworthy occasion or celebration that you want to throw for the pupils.

Pedagogical Practice #59

Assure the pupil that you will SING THE BIRTHDAY SONG for them in front of the other children in the classroom. It works wonderfully!

Pedagogical Practice #60

Encourage students' interest in studying with the NEW BUCKET LIST by rearranging the classroom's wall hangings, notices, charts, and other teaching aids in a haphazard manner.

Pedagogical Practice #61

Remembering the names of all of the students in your class by their FIRST NAMES can help you become a ROCKSTAR TEACHER. Never call your students by their ROLL NUMBERS or by the SIR NAME.

Pedagogical Practice #62

In order to get a better understanding of the child's approach to learning, at least once every SESSION, a visit to the child's home should be arranged in advance.

Pedagogical Practice #63

Make it a point to teach LIFE SKILLS in addition to the SUBJECT that you have been given responsibility for. Your pupils and you would have a unique relationship as a result of this activity. It's possible that "dwelling interest among them" will necessitate "discussing about MALALA and OBAMA."

Pedagogical Practice #64

Put on your favorite PERFUME and present yourself to your pupils as a dignified PERSONALITY by cultivating some personal branding. Students appreciate Street Smart Teachers!

Pedagogical Practice #65

Always look things up in some REFERENCE BOOKS, and don't just restrict yourself to the ones that are prescribed—this includes e-books and references found online.

Pedagogical Practice #66

Do not put yourself in a box that COMMENTS & WORDS OF PRAISE about viz. It is unacceptable for the sole criticism or comment on the Report Cards to be "CAN DO BETTER." PLEASE.

Pedagogical Practice #67

While taking attendance, as a CLASS TEACHER you should think about being innovative. Do not ever bolt a restricted proxy or a response code of YES SIR or PRESENT SIR. Instead, create some roll out prompts to ensure that it is communicated clearly and audibly.

Pedagogical Practice #68

Ask questions to which 90 percent of the students MAY have a response, not those to which they HAVE to have an answer. The objective should not be to embrace phobia; rather, it should be to connect.

Pedagogical Practice #69

The technique of QUALITY CIRCLE should be carried out in the classroom with a minimum of five people in each group. They are required to meet together, discuss the Pedagogical Practice, and then come up with some DATA, which will be followed by a PRESENTATION given by the group.

Pedagogical Practice #70

Encourage experiential learning in almost all of the disciplines that are taught so that students may acquire soft skills, decision making, and how to interact with nature.

Pedagogical Practice #71

Make sure that your BODY LANGUAGE is appropriate and that it is effectively expressed so that it does not provide any incorrect information to the kids. Even the NAIL PAINT that the professors wear is scrutinized by the children.

Pedagogical Practice #72

A TEACHER has a responsibility to respect the VARIOUS POINTS OF VIEW held by the pupils in their class. Every single student in the class should be acknowledged for the contributions they've made.

Pedagogical Practice #73

Utilizing technology in the classroom to maintain a connection with kids around the clock will help you become a ROCKSTAR TEACHER.
Increase the frequency with which you utilize your PEN DRIVE. Investigate the possibility of establishing a connection with your customers or target demographic by utilizing educational apps.

Pedagogical Practice #74

Have faith in your pupils and know that they are capable of great things with just a little bit of encouragement and acknowledgment from you. Consider them to be YOUNG ADULTS rather than children any more.

Pedagogical Practice #75

Consider your students to be your true superiors at all times. Keep in mind that you must appease more than 40 supervisors across five sectors each and every day. Always and first and foremost, wow them with your thoughtful considerations, your extensive knowledge, and your impeccable style.

Pedagogical Practice #76

Investigate the possibility of learning via COLLABORATIVE endeavors rather than through TEACHING, and ensure that you combine your educational pursuits with a pastime so that you may have DELIGHT in the process of sharing and learning. Instead of saying "Let me TEACH!," try using the words "Let us Learn." "

Pedagogical Practice #77

*Put a stop to the excessive use of certain terms.
During your time in the classroom, you should
use the phrases "TRY," "BUT," and "IF."
because they foster a mindset of pessimism.*

Pedagogical Practice #78

*Make use of references and works by other
writers in order to dispel the misconception that
students have, which is that "Sir, that is already
in the book; give us something new."*

Pedagogical Practice #79

*Establish a MILESTONE CHART as a top
priority for both the achievement of your pupils
and your own happiness.
Make sure that each and every one of your
pupils gets a perfect score in your class!*

Pedagogical Practice #80

Altering your tactics for BREAKING THE ICE and your interactive vocabulary is one way to periodically recalibrate both your behavior and your teaching abilities.

Pedagogical Practice #81

Be alert and awake at all times!
You should all have a pair of eyeballs in the back of your heads. Request that your pupils work together and share their Pedagogical Practices on the Facebook page associated with your classroom.

Pedagogical Practice #82

Pay attention to what they have to say and respond to their questions as you see fit.

Pedagogical Practice #83

Have faith in the win-win scenario and the OWNERSHIP way of thinking. My sons and daughters are the most amazing people ever! Winners are the ones that MAKE things happen, while losers are the ones who let things happen.

Pedagogical Practice #84

Never in public compare your work to that of other instructors or criticize them for their work, since the more you blame, the more ineffective you seem.

Pedagogical Practice #85

Recognize that you are not without flaws. Develop a routine that allows you to adapt to the passing of time. Put your student days in the past since you can't teach in the same way that you were taught. Forget about them!

Pedagogical Practice #86

Recognize that you are NOT PERFECT and own that fact.
Instead of seeing it as an uncommon event,

make learning to learn a habit in your life!

Pedagogical Practice #87

Investigate the
KWINK Analysis (Knowing What I Now Know)
and make an effort to work around both your
weaknesses and your strengths. Focus on your
shortcomings and use them as building blocks
for your future success by working on them.

Pedagogical Practice #88

Forget about it.
COMFORT ZONE
Take satisfaction in the obstacles you face and
the opportunity you have to teach other courses
or senior classes, organize opportunities for
involvement, and accept additional tasks.

Pedagogical Practice #89

Accept one hundred percent of the responsibility
for the outcome of your class and the overall

academic environment of the class. This is the foundation upon which your self-respect, self-esteem, self-confidence, and self-reliance are built.

Pedagogical Practice #90

Together with the kids and other employees, practice thinking positively.
ALL THE TIME
Because of this, you will develop knowledge inside yourself and rapport with your peers.

Pedagogical Practice #91

Gain experience in managing a classroom by applying the 80/20 rule to the many responsibilities and pursuits you face on a daily basis and determining your priorities accordingly. Keep in mind that just twenty percent of the things on your list will account for eighty percent of the outcomes you see. By establishing a Facebook Event, you can ensure that your students will remember to put your upcoming classroom event on their calendars.

Pedagogical Practice #92

Reduce the amount of distractions you cause within the classes. It is best to refrain from monitoring messages, calls, postings, or updates while you are in the classroom. A ready reckoner instructor who cares about their students would never even bring their cell phone into the classroom.

Pedagogical Practice #93

Carry yourself not like a RING MASTER but rather like a ZEN MASTER.
Instead of acting as a HARD TASK MASTER, you may consider letting the kids in the class follow your spiritual learning and blessings.

Pedagogical Practice #94

Be SMART! To be methodical in the classroom, meticulous in the workshop, artistic in the presentation, and realistic in the calibration of instruments.
Regarding the Management of the Classroom

Pedagogical Practice #95

Adjust your demeanor such that it better fits the dynamics of the educational environment. Never harbor resentment or hostility against any of the students, under any circumstances. Please accept my sincere apologies, and may the good Lord bless you in everything that you do.

Pedagogical Practice #96

Put an end to your reactive behavior. Instead, you should prioritize the tasks that need the most of your time and energy. Ask the students to just continue the debate on Facebook and then proceed with the lesson if you believe that the discussion time is really fascinating.

Pedagogical Practice #97

Integrate a process known as T-MAIL, which stands for Teachers' Mail Box.
A message to the instructor to discuss with them in confidence on a question or an experience.

Pedagogical Practice #98

Utilize the POST-IT NOTES on the following: walls of the classroom up against a name. Notes of encouragement or suggestions for the child's own growth might be included. Both from the instructor to the student and the student to the instructor!

Pedagogical Practice #99

Notebooks containing student conversations should be passed around the classroom to different students. This might be a personal, tiny note book that the students write to the instructor with a particular comment on their accomplishments and questions.

Pedagogical Practice #100:

Say "Good Morning" to One Another
On a more personal tone at get-together times and during the Assembly hours in order to establish connection with the pupils.

Pedagogical Practice #101

Participate at lunch and break times with the pupils by eating a meal with them. The children like to take turns cooking and eating, and they get a kick out of hearing compliments on how good the food tastes. They do this to foster trust and create relationships with one another.

Pedagogical Practice #102

Always give the impression that you are the TEACHER that you have always known you could be. Take a back seat in the classroom you're teaching in and act more like a student than a teacher. Make studying an everyday activity with the help of APPS like WORD OF THE DAY and THIS DAY IN HISTORY, which provide bite-sized educational morsels that are also entertaining.

Pedagogical Practice #103

One need to be encouraging the youngsters each and every time they are in the classroom. This should be done constantly. Give the impression that you are a ROCKSTAR to the children in the classroom by displaying some WOW elements.

Pedagogical Practice #104

Maintain a flexible approach to the decisions and assignments you hand out in the classroom, and give students the freedom to formulate their own opinions and organize their own bodies of knowledge.

Pedagogical Practice #105

Establish a 5S Quality Plan and action by installing the procedure.
Sorting, Cleaning, and Placing Into Classes

*Seiton; Straighten, Simplify, Set
in the appropriate manner, Setup
Sweep, shine, scrub, and clean up with seiso.
Clear the Air and Examine
Seiketsu; Standardize,
stabilize, Conformity
Shitsuke; Sustain, self
discipline, tradition and practice*

Pedagogical Practice #106

*The CANDO technique should be practiced on a
regular basis in the classroom.*
-
*Cleanup, Organization, Tidiness, Discipline,
and Continuous Enhancement*

Pedagogical Practice #107

*You should never be afraid to take calculated
risks, such as attending courses that are a
substitute, arrangement, or replacement for
another subject, or handling an assignment in a
new topic area.*

Pedagogical Practice #108

Never allow yourself to get caught up in regrets about previous mistakes or unwarranted musings on life lessons. You should have faith in your children's potential and match their self-assurance by creating learning opportunities for them via conversations and interactions.

Pedagogical Practice #109

Be careful not to repeat the same error repeatedly. It's possible that the pupils won't find you to be an entertaining instructor. Instead, you should approach them for support and assistance, especially in mapping out how to make use of technology in the classroom or other learning tools.

Pedagogical Practice #110

Expecting rapid results from your children is setting yourself up for disappointment. Maintain a high level of self-assurance and encourage positive behavior in the children by setting high standards for them and emphasizing a win-win strategy.

Pedagogical Practice #111

Do not resist change but rather embrace it and work to incorporate it on a regular basis. In the classroom, utilize the most advanced forms of technology with the help of the students. Remember, teachers are no longer the sages on the stage but the guides on the floor!

Pedagogical Practice #112

Master over your fears of classroom management and distractions within classrooms. Build a rapport with the children over time with your PERSONALITY and GOOD Vocabulary.

Pedagogical Practice #113

Always be willing to evolve as a Good Teacher with expertise to make learning happen and a difference every time you enter the classroom.

Pedagogical Practice #114

Cultivate a common interest in the class. Let all students prepare to learn with common objectives.

Pedagogical Practice #115

A sense of humour helps.

Pedagogical Practice #116

Never compare one child with the other in the class. No one wins the comparison game. Treat every child in the class as a Unique child with a different learning preference and a style.

Pedagogical Practice #117

Be a Rainmaker not just for the Class that you teach in, but also for the School where you work! The word "Rainmaker" was first used by Native Americans to refer to a medicine man who attempted to bring about precipitation via the performance of a variety of ceremonies and incantations.

Pedagogical Practice #118

First and foremost, you should act like a HUMAN BEING. Consider each and every youngster to be a fellow human being. Be human and take into account the current situation. Be sure to keep your homework assignments focused on human nature.

Pedagogical Practice #119

In addition to listening with your ears, you should also make it a point to watch the faces of the people in your audience as they respond to the questions you've posed. Pay attention with your whole body. Demonstrate your interest and send a message with your eyes. It's almost a given that excellent educators are also good listeners.

Pedagogical Practice #120

Make it a point to pose pertinent inquiries to the instructor throughout class and to repeat these inquiries in the form of questions on written or oral tests. They have to correspond to the information that is being taught and they can't be off limits for debate.

Pedagogical Practice #121

Maintain a state of readiness for any and all interactions, meetings, and presentations, as well as explanations. This is to convey a positive impression of your personality and teaching skills to the audience.

Pedagogical Practice #123

Pay close attention to your TOUCH TIME. And execute TIME MANAGEMENT that is effective throughout the discussions and the classroom project assignments.

Pedagogical Practice #124

It is essential for a Teacher to evaluate the Students' LEARNING OUTCOME after each and every Class. Following each session and module, do an analysis of the feedback received and any necessary course corrections.

Pedagogical Practice #125

As a TEACHER, you should always act as a Maven, which means you should accumulate information, a Connector, which means you should provide knowledge, and an Evangelist, which means you should cultivate followers and promote the notion that one may excel by sharing knowledge.

Pedagogical Practice #126

Quit Whining!

Over Arrangements, Substitutions, Replacement Classes, Attendance Register Updating, Extra Hours of Waiting, Teaching, and Meetings, as well as the Instruction of Young Boys and Girls in a Variety of Traits.

Pedagogical Practice #127

Master the art of refusing.
Do not be afraid to voice your disagreement when you believe it to be physically impossible to complete the work or the assignment. Never make false promises to children, especially ones that you believe are just cosmetic and have little chance of being kept.

Pedagogical Practice #128

Prepare a TO-DO List for the lessons you will be teaching in the classroom in accordance with the task or assignment you have scheduled for the week. Make the necessary preparations. Maintain a pleasant and inviting atmosphere conducive to learning in the classroom by ensuring that appropriate instructional resources are present and by assigning duties to individual students.

Pedagogical Practice #129

Always look for methods to do more with fewer steps as a teacher. Utilizing the power of technology, you should strive to be a multitasking individual.

and the backing of the other pupils. You could be instructing, watching, or commenting on a subject while at the same time doing a formative assessment in order to evaluate the children in the class in terms of their level of knowledge and their ability to behave appropriately.

Pedagogical Practice #130

exemplify courtesy and humility in every way. Respect for each and every kid in the classroom, together with a sense of modesty for the parents and other employees alike. Never be arrogant about your expertise, and always be willing to act as a ready reckoner for others.

Pedagogical Practice #131

Take the Initiative. Learn how tailor your classes and assignments to the preferences of the students, as well as how to handle the students' shifting emotions. With the pleasure of information sharing that is tailored to their own interests and preferences.

Pedagogical Practice #132

Never let go of your ability to learn, and always be well-prepared and organized with regard to the flow of both execution and thought. Sharing in order for the group to present it. Always go into a situation prepared, and with a positive attitude.

Pedagogical Practice #133

Leverage the potential of technology to extend communication beyond the parent-teacher conference. Use e-diaries, Make the most of enterprise resource planning (ERP) as well as other communication mediums in order to enlighten pupils in the classroom about their win-win characteristics.

Pedagogical Practice #134

Have a lovely planner available for the students in the lesson. The students like seeing concepts and colorful graphics that are mentioned as TO DO Things in the classroom. The term "innovation" what it is about creation and activation that people adore.

Pedagogical Practice #135

Maintain a well-organized and color-coded classroom that offers a wide variety of educational opportunities. Tools, charts, and visual representations It is important that the classroom be an engaging and stimulating environment.

Pedagogical Practice #136

Have position management: there should be a place for everything, and that location should include everything.

Pedagogical Practice #137

A TOOL BOX is an essential item that should be kept in every classroom by the instructor. A ready reckoner stocked with various items, which may include more chalk, a duster, charts, learning materials, and reference books.

Pedagogical Practice #138

The instructors are obligated to advise the students to concentrate on what is of the utmost significance on a consistent basis.

Pedagogical Practice #139

Unleash the master that lies dormant within you and provide the notion with the greatest explanation you can think of using all of your talents. Never be flippant about things, and unless absolutely necessary, steer out of the classroom. You should encourage the children to talk among themselves about a recent event like the football game that took place yesterday.

Pedagogical Practice #140

Become an expert in the art of telling stories. The pupils adore and value the opportunities to learn via tales and real-life occurrences. This makes an imprint and an impact on their thoughts that will endure forever, along with a lesson!

Pedagogical Practice #141

Have a Conversation, and be sure to rehearse consistently and thoroughly, as well as to absorb the material, so that you can present the discussion with the same ease as if you were conversing with a close friend.

Pedagogical Practice #142

It is important to have regular Class Assemblies in order to develop the children's spiritual quotient and to share meaningful content with them. Because of this, they are better able to control their emotions.

Pedagogical Practice #143

Create a CLASS Library consisting of a few reference books that will be available for students to borrow during class time. When they are allowed to access them at their own discretion and when necessary during the process of learning, it is always quite beneficial.

Pedagogical Practice #144

Introduce any item from the outside into the classroom in order to pique the students' interest and force them to learn about the item via the medium of a quiz.

Pedagogical Practice #145

As an alternative, you may enter your classroom dressed differently than you would on a typical day in order to transfer information and capture the attention of your pupils.

Pedagogical Practice #146

Make appropriate adjustments to both your volume and pitch depending on the topics that are being discussed in the group setting.

Pedagogical Practice #147

Find the youngster in your class who seems to be the least interested in the issue being discussed in class and ask him for his thoughts on the subject matter.

Pedagogical Practice #148

Your lesson should begin with a statement or phrases that are novel and attention-grabbing, such A passage from the Harry Potter books!

Pedagogical Practice #149

It is necessary to investigate and understand how to use free will responsibly in the classroom so that the pupils may model their behavior after yours.

Pedagogical Practice #150

Relaxed conversation should be maintained with the students both within the classroom and elsewhere on the campus. Make regular pauses and check to see if the person listening on the other end is doing so without showing any signs of fear or disinterest. Keep up with the progress that the pupils are making.

Pedagogical Practice #151

You should often encourage your pupils to share what they have learned with others.

Pedagogical Practice #152

Students should be required to engage in their own education during each and every course via the use of assignments, survey forms, and oral tests.

Pedagogical Practice #153

To facilitate learning with enthusiasm and dedication via workshops, webinars, and skype sessions, foster analytical thinking and active engagement among participants.

Pedagogical Practice #154

Allow your pupils to serve as a MODEL for you as a teacher.
Exercise Joy, Fun, and the Pursuit of Perfection.

Pedagogical Practice #155

Always begin with the. INTIMATION to kids about the subject matter, what it is that they are going to learn, teach them, let them practice it, and then ask them what they have learned. Prioritizing the discussion of assignments before winding down the session is essential.

Pedagogical Practice #156

Alter the flow of activity in the classroom by putting students in different groups. As a teacher, it is essential that you maintain complete control over the students' pairings.

Pedagogical Practice #157

Always establish parameters before beginning a work. Simply put, do not give them the opportunity to TRY at their own leisure. An assignment within a certain amount of time and a timely submission need to be a priority, and this goal should be shared by everyone.

Pedagogical Practice #158

Always be on the lookout for telltale indicators of boredom in your students, and adjust your instructional approach appropriately. If you see students "sleeping with their eyes open," you need to call an immediate halt to the lecture. "

Pedagogical Practice #159

Condense your thoughts on the Students in order to avoid making indirect criticism and focusing on an inability to learn in any other way.

Pedagogical Practice #160

Realize that no one enjoys being around gloomy individuals, and that your students' observations of you as a lazy instructor would have a detrimental impact on their desire in learning.

Pedagogical Practice #161

Instead of giving each student an individual work, keep your pupils occupied by giving them group assignments. Ask them to construct genuine projects so that they may be utilized in other classrooms or later in life. This will prepare them for the real world.

Pedagogical Practice #162

Have a video recording of the session in the classroom when a particular or challenging subject was discussed. Taking a look at previously learned material with fresh eyes could prove to be beneficial in this regard. After it has been uploaded, it could also be used as a ready reckoner online!

Pedagogical Practice #163

Stop Arguing and causing trouble. Let it go approach may be the best for you as a TEACHER. Forgive and Forget.

Pedagogical Practice #164

Share the learning from attending an SKILL DEVELOPMENT workshop or share the learning you have had with the colleagues in the recent "Enrichment Meeting"

Pedagogical Practice #165

Take a break! Get the best out of yourself with sports or singing a song to make a lively environment filled with comic and entertainment within the classroom.

Pedagogical Practice #166

Take a Qualification using some of the online resources and make it public the students. Give them the option to follow your learning.

Pedagogical Practice #167

Use links like SCRIBD.COM for sharing Pedagogical Practices/ concepts/ write-ups and get a follow stream at a 24x4 approach. Avoid social networking connectivity.

Pedagogical Practice #168

Carry your smile always. If you see someone without a smile, give them one of yours!

Pedagogical Practice #169

Love your students and make them feel they are the most important people for you. This brings their liking for you and their being in the classrooms.

Pedagogical Practice #170

Assume your students to be the best children in the world. With no comparison so at all. Compare them with themselves of yesterday and the next day they should and would be!

Pedagogical Practice #171

Assume that your students are the best of the students in the world. Meet to their expectations by delivering the best and make them feel so by giving them hour, recognition and pride. Praise what and when you can!

Pedagogical Practice #172

Display the classroom rules and enforce them consistently. Never let it go without practice.

Pedagogical Practice #173

Use positive language with no negative words and negative belief. Be win-win all the time, every time.

•

Pedagogical Practice #174

Make your students responsible for their own learning environment. Let them question the learning with no fear of failure but an encourage participation by all.

Pedagogical Practice #175

Make it a point to avoid confrontations in front of the students in class. Let it roll with peace and prosperity of understanding.

Pedagogical Practice #176

Connect with the Parents through the students and they must be informed about the connect. The fear is natural and let that be there.

Pedagogical Practice #177

Assure and assume the Attention of every student in the class before the lesson begins. This may be done using ICE BREAKERS or using pointers of easy questions which 90% of the students may answer!

Pedagogical Practice #178

Always use simple verbal reprimands but in PRIVATE when the misbehavior occurs. This leads to understanding the child and his modeling of the behavior is achieved.

Pedagogical Practice #179

*Avoid the threats like
"I shall call your parents" or
"I shall take you to the PRINCIPAL"
This dilutes your importance and recognition.*

Pedagogical Practice #180

Do intervene as soon as possible for any even if, a trivial matter of misbehavior among the children in class. Ignoring means enhancing the trouble.

Pedagogical Practice #181

Let the students learn to strive for greater self-control during situational analysis within classrooms.

Pedagogical Practice #182

Activate a ROLE PLAY based learning and knowledge. Make the maximum participation possible by the students.

Pedagogical Practice #183

Never get emotional with any student in class. Your profession is of a TEACHER and not simply a PARENT. You need to occupy spectrum of discipline with AWE- Respect with Fear- on Demand!

Pedagogical Practice #184

Spend so much time improving yourself that you have no time for staff Room politics and to criticize others. Believe in your wisdom towards excellence!

Pedagogical Practice #185

Be so strong with your words and commitment that nothing can disturb your peace of mind in the classroom and in the school. Stay away from classroom distractions instead try implementing solutions to every concern in the class.

Pedagogical Practice #186

Talk health, happiness and hygiene towards prosperity to every student you meet. Make them feel good every time they meet you. Inspire *them with good words, motivation and inspiration.*

Pedagogical Practice #187

Have a dedicated time for PEP TALK, ASSEMBLY TALK and above all some ZEN Talk with the students on life, living and wisdom! Discussion realities attached to LIFE as a Mystery!

Pedagogical Practice #188

Be as enthusiastic about the success of each and every student of yours as you are for yourself. Make the recognition public via all means of sharing including SOCIAL MEDIA. It counts!

Pedagogical Practice #189

Activate CLASS WISE Assembly and invite the parents to witness the same with participation of each and every student of the class.

Pedagogical Practice #190

Invite PARENTS for FAMILY HOUR once a month for 10 minutes ONE TO ONE with you and the other subject Teachers together with the Child and give him praises of count and wisdom.

Pedagogical Practice #191

Send PRAISES to parents whose students perform good out of average. Send them Congratulations Card and tag them as a WINNER Parent of the week! On the school's FB Page.

Pedagogical Practice #192

Once a week ask your children to write a love letter to themselves. Praising them for their great doings and acknowledging their wrong doings. Make them read and share the findings with their friends.

Pedagogical Practice #193

Make the classroom routine routed with the phrases:
I can I will I care All I want is within me, I am confident, I can do it, YES!

Pedagogical Practice #194

Ability comes from doing and not WATCHING. As a teacher let this happen in classrooms through role plays, experiential learning and participative learning.

Pedagogical Practice #195

Encourage COMPETENCY Not COMPETITION. Let the competency of individuals be explored via formative assessments routed and guided by the teachers.

Pedagogical Practice #196

Happy Teachers Change the world of learning in the classrooms. Be happy and excited with every moment of joy and replicate that in your children while teaching. Develop your HAPPINESS QUOTIENT.

Pedagogical Practice #197

WHO and HOW you are educates the child more than what you teach. Make your presence felt and explored in class by your attributes.

Pedagogical Practice #198

Don't Walk the talk, Don't Talk the talk, Instead WORK The talk!

Pedagogical Practice #199

Treat every classroom As A LEARNING WALK! Never take arrangement or substitution classes as a liability instead, make it a learning

Opportunity for the kids!

ABOUT THE AUTHOR

Dheeraj Mehrotra, MS, MPhil, PhD (Education Management) honoris causa., a white and a yellow belt in SIX SIGMA, a Certified NLP Business Diploma holder, is an Educational Innovator, Author, with expertise in Six Sigma In Education, Academic Audits, Neuro-Linguistic Programming (NLP), Total Quality Management In Education, an Experiential Educator, a CBSE Resource towards School Assessment (SQAA), CCE, JIT, Five S, and KAIZEN.

He has authored over 100 books on topics which include Computer Science, AI, Digital Body Language, NLP, Quality Circles, School Management, Classroom Effectiveness and Safety and security in schools. A former Principal at De Indian Public School, New Delhi, (INDIA), NPS International School, Guwahati, and Education Officer at GEMS, Gurgaon, with an ample teaching experience of over Two Decades, he is a certified Trainer for Quality Circles/ TQM in Education and QCI Standards for School Accreditation/ School Audits and Management.

He has also been honoured with the President

of India's National Teacher Award in the year 2006 and the Best Science Teacher State Award (By the Ministry of Science and Technology, State of UP), Innovation in Education for his inception of Six Sigma In Education by Education Watch, New Delhi and Education World- Best Teacher Award, BOLT Learner Teacher Award by Air India, 'Innovation in Education Award 2016' by Higher Education Forum (HEF), Gujarat Chapter, among others. He has developed over 150 FREE EDUCATIONAL MOBILE Apps for the Google Play Store exclusively for Teachers, Students, and Parents. This work has been recognised by the LIMCA BOOK OF RECORDS & INDIA BOOK OF RECORDS as the only Indian to draw that feast. Dr Mehrotra works as a PRINCIPAL at KUNWARS GLOBAL SCHOOL, Lucknow, in India.

He has conducted over 1000 workshops globally on "Excellence In Education" integrated with Total Quality Management and Six Sigma, Technology Integration in Education (TIE), Developing towards being ROCKSTAR TEACHERS, including Cyberspace, Cyber Security, Classroom Management, School Leadership & Management, and Innovative teaching within classrooms via Mind Maps, NLP and Experiential Learning in Academics. He is an active TEDx speaker and can be viewed on the youtube TEDx channel.

As a premium UDEMY Instructor, he has developed over 450 courses and caters to over 8 Lakh students from 180 countries.

He can be visited at www.authordheerajmehrotra.com.

BASICS OF
ARTIFICIAL
INTELLIGENCE
&
MACHINE
LEARNING
DR. DHEERAJ MEHROTRA
authordheerajmehrotra.com
Flipkart
available at
amazon
BY NATIONAL
AWARDEE
EDUCATOR
Digital List Price: ₹103.95
Kindle Price: ₹99.00
Save ₹4.95 (4%)
inclusive of all taxes

BY NATIONAL
AWARDEE
EDUCATOR
Kindle Price: ₹ 72.00
inclusive of all taxes
Teaching in the VUCA WORLD
Dr. Dheeraj Mehrotra
authordheerajmehrotra.com
Flipkart
available at
amazon

101
SCHOOL
MANAGEMENT
STRATEGIES
Towards EFFECTIVE
QUALITY MANAGEMENT
System in Schools
DR. DHEERAJ
MEHROTRA
Digital List Price: ₹72.45
M.R.P.: ₹199.00
Kindle Price: ₹ 69.00
Save ₹ 130.00 (65%)
inclusive of all taxes
amazon
www.authordheerajmehrotra.com

FOR KIDS
OF ALL
AGES
Maximizing
Learning
Potential of
Kids
CODING
FOR
KIDS IN
PYTHON
DR DHEERAJ
MEHROTRA
Rs. 199/-
amazon
www.authordheerajmehrotra.com

available at
amazon
150/-
Teacher's
Guide To
Coding In
Schools
Dr Dheeraj Mehrotra

BY NATIONAL AWARDEE EDUCATOR
DR. DHEERAJ MEHROTRA
EXPERIENTIAL LEARNING FOR EDUCATORS
TOWARDS QUALITY LITERACY FOR ALL
NOW AVAILABLE AT
amazon
authordheerajmehrotra.com

www.ingramcontent.com/pod-product-compliance
Lightning Source LLC
Chambersburg PA
CBHW020326180726

47991CB00019B/984